UNSTOPPABLE STARTS HERE

A Short Guide to Mastering Your Brain and Unlocking Your Life

Also by Roddy Carter

BodyWHealth: Journey to Abundance

Sunset Lessons: Reflections on Light and Love from the Darkest of Places

Fireside Wisdom: Conversations to Inspire Personal Mastery

The Problem With Anger: And How to Solve It

Becoming Unstoppable: Your Neurocentric Coaching Guide to Achieving Unstoppable Success

The Serpent Within: Navigating Fear to Restore Inner Harmony

The Problem With Suffering: And the Science of Hope

Unstoppable You Online Courses
(available from www.roddycarter.com):
Unstoppable You
Unstoppable You Business
Unleash Unstoppable
Unleash Success

UNSTOPPABLE STARTS HERE

A Short Guide to Mastering Your Brain and Unlocking Your Life

Roddy Carter, MD

Aquila Life Science Press
La Jolla, California

FIRST AQUILA LIFE SCIENCE PRESS EDITION, JUNE 2025
Published by Aquila Life Science, LLC, La Jolla, CA

UNSTOPPABLE STARTS HERE.

ISBN: 979-8-9990257-0-8

Printed in the United States of America

For every brave soul who senses there is more—
more within you, more ahead of you,
more meant for you.

This book is your road map,
not because you are lost,
but because you are ready to arrive.

Introduction

Why You're Not Broken

Most people arrive at this moment silently: successful on the outside but stuck on the inside. Their momentum fades. Their clarity fogs. They hesitate when they used to charge ahead.

If that's you, take a breath. You're in exactly the right place.

And you're also not broken. You're not lazy. You're not failing.

You're simply running a powerful biological system—your brain—without a user's manual. And for high achievers like you, that system can eventually work against you, not because you're weak but because you've outgrown the strategies that once kept you safe.

This short guide is your map to freedom. Freedom not from effort, but from confusion. From hustle without direction. From performance that costs you your peace. It's time to update the operating system that drives everything in your life.

Inside these pages, you'll

- Discover the five essential regions of your brain and how they shape every thought, choice, and feeling you have.

- Learn why fear (not failure) is the true barrier to your next breakthrough.

- Reclaim the driver's seat of your own mind and future.

You won't find fluff. You'll find precision, compassion, and clear neuroscience explained in human terms. You'll find a wake-up call for your potential.

And it all begins here, where you realize you were never the problem. You just needed the right instructions.

Let's begin.

Chapter 1

Journey Toward Unstoppable

Becoming *unstoppable* doesn't mean pushing harder. It means aligning deeper.

Most of us were taught that success comes from doing more: more work, more hustle, more sacrifice. And for a while, that probably worked. You advanced. You delivered. You led.

But then something changed. Quietly.

You began to feel like you were spinning your wheels. The clarity that once guided you faded. You started questioning decisions that used to come easily. You still look successful, but inside, you know something's off.

That's because the version of you who succeeded isn't the version of you who will rise to the next level.

The next version of you—the *unstoppable* you—requires a different kind of mastery. Not just over your time or habits, but over the operating system of your life: your brain.

This chapter is your invitation to begin that journey. It's not about changing who you are. It's about returning to who you were before the world taught you to adapt and survive.

And it starts with one powerful question: What does your ideal future look like?

Not the ideal future society expects. Not the one your résumé reflects. But the one that would make you feel alive, fulfilled, and free.

Pause here. Take a deep breath. Let it rise.

You don't need to have every detail figured out, but even a glimpse of that future creates momentum. It calls your brain forward. It reorients your inner compass.

We'll revisit this ideal future again soon. But for now, just know: You're on the edge of reinvention. And this time, it will be led from within.

Chapter 2

Your Brain Operating System

Most people think their brain is one thing, one voice, one mind.

But that's not how it works.

Inside your head, there's a whole team of regions and structures—each with its own voice, strengths, and agenda. Some are ancient and instinctual. Others are newer and more refined. Together, they create your experience of life: how you think, feel, act, react, and decide.

I call this system your *Brain Operating System*, or *BOS* for short.

When you understand your BOS, life starts making more sense. You see why you sometimes sabotage your own goals, why fear shows up in disguise, and why your motivation rises and falls. You stop blaming yourself and start gaining authority.

Let's meet your BOS team:

- *The Reptilian Brain:* This is your survival system. It keeps you alive, but it doesn't care whether you're happy. It reacts fast, often with fear or withdrawal.

- *The Emotional Brain:* This part helps you connect, love, and belong. It feels deeply, but it can also overreact if unregulated.

- *The Cognitive Brain:* This is your rational thinker. It analyzes, plans, and organizes, but it can become paralyzed by complexity.

- *The Prefrontal Cortex:* This is where your conscious leadership lives, your "internal CEO." It's the only part of your brain that can see the whole picture.

- *The Attention Focusing Consortium (AFC):* This cluster of brain regions acts as an internal filter, deciding what you notice and what you ignore.

Each part plays a role, but here's the challenge: If you don't consciously lead via your prefrontal cortex, your reptilian brain will always take over.

It will run your life reactively. It will make decisions out of fear. It will keep you in habits and loops that once kept you safe but now just keep you stuck.

This is the hidden reason so many high achievers feel like they're "off": They've upgraded their lives, but they're still running the same outdated brain patterns.

Here's the good news: You can update your BOS. And it doesn't require rewiring your entire life. Just one insight, one shift, or one practice at a time is enough to make a meaningful difference.

In the next chapter, we'll explore the most powerful override system in your brain and how fear keeps hijacking it when you need it most.

For now, remember: You have more power than you could reasonably imagine.

Your Practice

Pause and reflect on these questions:

- *Which brain regions do you think are currently running your day?*

- *Are you reacting or leading?*

Which brain regions do you think are currently running your day?

_____

_____

_____

_____

_____

_____

_____

_____

_____

Are you reacting or leading?

_____

_____

_____

_____

_____

_____

_____

_____

_____

_____

Chapter 3

The Fear Filter

Fear doesn't always shout. Sometimes, it whispers. It shows up disguised as logic, busyness, indecision, or the urge to play it safe.

The brain's primary directive is survival—not success. This means that fear, biologically, always gets the first word...and often the last word. The issue is that fear is programmed to dominate, and it regularly oversteps. It starts making decisions that aren't about safety; they're about comfort.

The problem with that? Comfort is the enemy of growth.

You don't need to get rid of fear. You need to understand its role, recognize its patterns, and take back the steering wheel.

Let's look at how fear shows up:

- *Avoidance:* "I'll do it later."

- *Overthinking:* "What if I make the wrong choice?"

- *Perfectionism:* "It has to be perfect before I begin."

- *Distraction:* "I'm just so busy right now."

- *Deferral to Others:* "Let me see what they think first."

Each of these voices sounds reasonable, but they're rooted in fear that is often just subtle resistance to vulnerability, exposure, or change.

Here's the truth: Fear is not the enemy. *Unquestioned* fear is.

When you notice your fear and stay present, you regain choice. You can choose courage—not recklessness, but intentional bravery rooted in clarity.

Client Story: The Courage to Move

A client named James came to me after months of spinning his wheels in a job that had long stopped inspiring him. He'd convinced himself it was not the right time to make a change. His résumé was polished and his LinkedIn connections were growing, but he never hit "send" on applications.

Through our work together, James realized that, behind the excuses of busyness, was fear disguised as logic. What if he failed? What if he wasn't good enough?

When he finally named those fears, they shrank. He took a small step forward. Then another. Within three months, he was working in a role that lit him up. And the voice of fear? Well, it didn't disappear, but it no longer ruled the room.

Here's a simple practice to overcome fear:

1. *Pause* when you feel resistance.

2. *Name* the voice of fear: "This is the voice of delay" or "This is the voice of distraction."

3. *Ask:* Is this keeping me safe or keeping me small?

4. *Breathe:* Inhale deeply, pause to center yourself, and exhale as though you are expelling the fear.

5. *Act* from alignment with your deliberate intention.

Your Practice

Pause and reflect on these questions:

- *Where do you notice fear disguised as logic in your life?*

- *What is one area where fear might be holding the mic?*

- *This week, what small, courageous act can you take—even while fear is present—toward your dream life?*

Where do you notice fear disguised as logic in your life?

_____

_____

_____

_____

_____

_____

_____

_____

_____

_____

What is one area where fear might be holding the mic?

_____

_____

_____

_____

_____

_____

_____

_____

_____

_____

This week, what small, courageous act can you take—even while fear is present—toward your dream life?

_____

_____

_____

_____

_____

_____

_____

_____

_____

_____

_____

Chapter 4

Own the Office of the CEO

Inside your brain is a quiet, powerful command center. It's called your *prefrontal cortex*, and it's where your wisest leadership lives. It's not loud. It doesn't push. But when it's online, everything changes.

The prefrontal cortex is the only part of your brain that can

- Zoom out and see the full picture;
- Pause before reacting;
- Imagine future consequences; and
- Choose values over impulses.

It's what allows you to lead *yourself.*

I call it the "Office of the CEO" because that's the role it plays. It integrates data from all other brain regions and makes strategic decisions. But—like any CEO—it can't function if you're constantly interrupted by chaos.

Here's the problem: When fear takes over, you get kicked out of the Office of the CEO.

Your survival systems (especially the reptilian and emotional brains) can overwhelm your CEO voice in milliseconds—before you notice. They aren't evil; they're just doing their job: protecting you. But they're not designed for long-term strategy. They're designed for escape from imminent threat.

To live and lead from the Office of the CEO, you must learn how to

- Notice when you've dropped into fear;
- Re-center intentionally; and
- Reclaim your authority.

Here's a five-minute CEO reboot you can use:

1. **Sit or stand tall**. Own your posture.

2. **Breathe deeply**, in through your nose and out through your mouth.

3. Place your hand on your heart to **feel your presence**.

4. **Name your current state**: "I am in fear" or "I feel foggy."

5. **Declare your leadership**: "I choose to lead from clarity."

This may sound simple, but your brain is listening. And the more often you activate this ritual, the easier it becomes to lead with awareness.

Your CEO voice isn't always the loudest in the room, but it's the one that creates your future.

Client Story: Leading Through Uncertainty

A client I worked with—let's call her Amara—was navigating a major decision: whether to step down from her executive role to pursue work more aligned with her inner north star. Her emotional brain was activated, concerned about identity, income, and legacy. Her reptilian brain had overloaded her cognitive brain with what-ifs.

But after practicing the CEO reboot daily, Amara experienced a subtle but powerful shift. "One morning," she said, "I finally heard the part of me that wasn't afraid. Just wise." That voice didn't shout. It led. Calmly and clearly, it pointed her toward alignment.

She took the leap. And for the first time in years, she didn't feel scattered—she

---

felt sovereign. The rest was easy, and now she's working in a deeply fulfilling leadership role leading an organization that improves hundreds of lives every day.

Your Practice

Try the CEO reboot for three days in a row. Then, pause and reflect on these questions:

- *What changed in your tone, decisions, or body language?*

- *Can you hear your inner wise leader, who has been waiting to be heard?*

Chapter 5

Build Belief

You've reclaimed your seat in the Office of the CEO. Now it's time to build the foundation that makes forward motion possible: belief.

Belief is not wishful thinking. It's a biological force. Every thought you repeat sends signals through your brain and body, shaping your patterns, postures, emotions, and outcomes.

Your brain is an incredible prediction engine. It constantly searches for patterns to believe in. If you tell it something long enough—especially if it's loaded with emotion—it begins to code that story into your identity.

The story you tell yourself becomes the life you live.

This means that self-doubt isn't just a mindset. It's a pattern—one you've practiced unconsciously.

And belief? That's a pattern, too.

Let's be clear: Believing in yourself doesn't mean you ignore your limitations. It means you trust in your capacity to learn, adapt, and grow. It means you stop outsourcing your worth to past results.

Here's how to build belief, from a neurocentric standpoint:

1. ***Inventory your assets.*** List your strengths and gifts—not titles or achievements, but personal traits.

2. ***Practice gratitude for your gifts.*** Appreciation increases your brain's receptivity to possibility.

3. ***Choose new thoughts on purpose.*** Pick one or two intentional beliefs to practice daily.

4. ***Reinforce with emotion.*** Speak these beliefs out loud. Let your body rehearse what your brain is learning.

5. ***Expand with movement.*** Practice power poses—confident, expansive physical stances that signal strength to your brain—daily to activate the body-brain loop and boost your belief system.

These are not affirmations. They are commands to your operating system delivered in your CEO voice.

Your beliefs are not fixed. They're programmable.

Client Story: The Breakthrough on the Track

A client of mine—let's call him Lucas— was a gifted sprinter, teetering on the edge of the international stage. He had the physical ability. His times were competitive. His coaches believed in him. But something subtle kept him from crossing the threshold into greatness.

He'd choke under pressure—not dramatically, but just enough. A slow start. A misstep on the curve. A final surge that came seconds too late. Over and over again, his performances plateaued: brilliant in training, but muted on race day.

In our work together, we uncovered the real barrier: Lucas didn't fully believe he belonged at the top. His inner voice, conditioned by years of self-comparison and near-misses, had begun to whisper that he was a contender but not a champion.

So, we didn't start with his stride. We started with his story.

Through visualization work, we retrained his brain to recognize a different narrative. He practiced seeing himself dominate the race—feeling the rhythm, hearing the roar of the crowd, savoring the surge across the finish line. He didn't just imagine success; he *rehearsed* it, with emotion and intention.

Three months later, at a major meet, Lucas ran a personal best...and placed first against an international field.

He later told me, "The biggest change wasn't in my legs. It was in my mind. I finally ran the race I had already seen a hundred times in my head."

Your Practice

Pause and reflect on these questions:

- *What does your unstoppable self already know?*

- *When you close your eyes, what is the boldest vision of your future that comes alive?*

- *What is one powerful belief you're ready to practice daily?*

What does your unstoppable *self already know?*

_____

_____

_____

_____

_____

_____

_____

_____

_____

When you close your eyes, what is the boldest vision of your future that comes alive?

_____

_____

_____

_____

_____

_____

_____

_____

_____

_____

What is one powerful belief you're ready to practice daily?

_____

_____

_____

_____

_____

_____

_____

_____

_____

_____

Chapter 6

Activate Your Desire

Desire is not a luxury. It's fuel.

It's the emotional energy that powers your beliefs into motion. Without it, even the most aligned plans stall. But with it? Your life starts to feel magnetized. Energized. Alive.

Many high performers have unintentionally shut down desire. Why? Because desire can feel risky. It opens you to disappointment. It reminds you of what you *don't* yet have. But here's the twist: Your emotion boosts you either forward or backward. So, if it's not boosting you forward, it's boosting you backward.

When you reconnect with desire, you awaken a powerful motivational loop in the brain—a connection between your emotional centers and your action systems.

What you *long* for is what leads you.

Let's bring your motivation back online with these steps to reignite desire in the brain:

1. **Name what you want.** Let it be honest. Let it be yours. Don't just name what's safe or practical but what would truly move you. Big or small, specific or vague—just begin.

2. **Use emotional language.** Desire is rooted in the emotional brain. So, use feeling words:

   - "I will feel proud."

   - "I will feel freedom in my body."

   - "I will wake up excited again."

3. **Visualize with sensory detail.** Don't just think it: See it, hear it, feel it, smell it, and taste it. The more sensory input you add, the more your brain encodes it as real.

4. **Move toward it daily.** Tiny steps count. Desire strengthens when paired with consistent, conscious action.

Desire isn't childish; it's catalytic. It infuses emotion into intention, amplifying your CEO voice to chart the path forward and energizing your BOS to execute that mission with purpose and power.

Client Story: Permission to Want More

One client—Elena—had built a beautiful life with a thriving business and a supportive, loving family. Yet she came to me feeling strangely restless. "I should be content," she said. "But something's missing."

Through our work, she realized she had stopped allowing herself to want. Somewhere along the way, desire had become a liability—something to suppress, not honor.

When she gave herself permission to explore her longing—creative expression, deeper friendships, a sloweddown lifestyle—everything changed. She didn't burn it all down. She simply began weaving new threads of aliveness into her current life. And that, she said, was more fulfilling than any success she'd had before.

Your desire is wisdom. Trust it to guide you home.

Your Practice

Pause and reflect on these questions:

- *If you weren't afraid of seeming ungrateful or unrealistic, what would you admit you deeply want?*

- *What feeling are you craving more of in your day-to-day life?*

- *What's one tiny action you could take this week that honors that desire?*

If you weren't afraid of seeming ungrateful or unrealistic, what would you admit you deeply want?

_____

_____

_____

_____

_____

_____

_____

_____

_____

_____

What feeling are you craving more of in your day-to-day life?

_____

_____

_____

_____

_____

_____

_____

_____

_____

_____

What's one tiny action you could take this week that honors that desire?

Chapter 7

Make Commitments

Desire fuels the journey. But *commitment* makes it real.

Commitment is not about rigidity or perfection. It's about alignment. It's a promise you make to your future self—and a pattern you reinforce every time you show up.

In the brain, commitment activates a network of focus, motivation, and emotional alignment. When you make a clear commitment, your BOS begins to filter for cues and actions that support it.

And here's the nuance: Real commitment is not about doing more. It's about deciding who you are becoming and backing it with your behavior.

The self you commit to becomes the self you embody.

Here's how to craft a neurocentric commitment:

1. ***Define your identity-based goal.*** Don't just commit to actions. Commit to becoming. Here are some examples:

    - "I commit to becoming someone who leads with calm clarity."

    - "I commit to becoming a person who honors my energy and time."

2. ***Clarify the "why."*** Who do you want to become? What do you want your life to look like? Link your commitment to your ideal future. Make it meaningful. Make it yours.

3. ***Create rituals, not rules.*** Rituals anchor behavior in rhythm, not rigidity. Identify one small, symbolic action to begin reinforcing the commitment.

4. ***Track identity wins.*** Each day, ask, "How did I embody my commitment to my future self, today?"

5. ***Honor the lapses.*** They aren't failures. They're feedback. Real commitment includes recommitment.

Commitment is the closing loop of the BOS cycle: from vision to belief to desire to action to identity.

And when you commit deeply, something remarkable happens: Your brain begins to believe that your future self is already real.

Your Practice

Pause and reflect on these questions:

- *Who are you becoming right now— by habit or by choice?*

- *Is it the one you want to be?*

- *What is one meaningful commitment you're ready to make to your future self?*

- *What small action can you ritualize to reinforce it, starting today?*

Who are you becoming right now—by habit or by choice?

_____

_____

_____

_____

_____

_____

_____

_____

_____

_____

Is it the one you want to be?

*What is one meaningful commitment you're ready
to make to your future self?*

_____

_____

_____

_____

_____

_____

_____

_____

_____

What small action can you ritualize to reinforce it, starting today?

Conclusion

What Happens Next

Becoming *unstoppable* is not about adding more pressure or chasing higher performance. It's about uncovering more truth, more clarity, and more alignment. Performance will follow!

You've just taken a powerful first step.

Along the way, you've met your BOS—no longer a mystery, but a map. You've seen how fear can quietly steer your choices, and you've learned how to lead from the Office of the CEO. You've explored belief, desire, and commitment, the deep drivers of meaningful change.

Most importantly, you've started something essential: You've reclaimed your role as the architect and builder of your own life.

That alone is transformational. And while this book has given you key insights and practices, it's just the beginning of what's possible.

I've created an online coaching program designed to take you deeper, guiding you through 10 immersive sessions that will bring your learning to life. The *Unstoppable You* digital coaching program is your next step to practical yet dramatic transformation.

Throughout the coaching experience, you'll

- Deepen your mastery of your BOS;

- Dismantle outdated patterns while practicing real-time rewiring;

- Build habits that align your inner world with your greatest goals; and

- Step fully into the identity of your *unstoppable* self.

True transformation isn't a one-time shift. It's a process—a return, again and again, to the deepest part of you, that's wise, courageous, and whole.

With each of these growth spurts, you are not starting over—you are starting from a new level of awareness and competence.

I see how those who step forward quickly are rewarded with rapid growth, while those who hesitate often faulter, even regress. So, let's keep going, right away. Use the wind you feel in your sails right now!

Scan the QR code above or visit me at roddycarter. com/unstoppable-starts-here to continue your surge toward *unstoppable*!

The next chapter of your journey is within your reach—and I'd be honored to walk it with you.

> If this book resonated with you, I'd be honored if you'd leave a review on the site where you purchased it...your voice helps others find it.